JEWISH
Humour

Other humour books from Prion

High Society by Michael Powell
The Ruling Asses by Stephen Robins
The Cynic's Dictionary by Aubrey Malone
Women's Wicked Wit by Michelle Lovric
Hollywood Wit by Rosemarie Jarski
Wisecracks by Rosemarie Jarski
The Languid Goat is Always Thin by Stephen Arnott
Do Unto Others …Then Run by Gerd de Ley
and David Potter
Funny Money by Michael Powell

Des MacHale's famous humorous quotations series:
Wit
Wit Hits the Spot
Wit on Target
Wit the Last Laugh
Wit Rides Again
Ultimate Wit
Irish Wit

JEWISH
Humour

BEN ELIEZER

PRION

First published in 2003 by
Prion Books
An imprint of the
Carlton Publishing Group
20 Mortimer Street
London
W1T 3JW

ISBN 1-85375-496-X

A catalogue record of this book is available from the
British Library

Cover design by Grade Design Consultants
Printed in Great Britain
by Mackays

With thanks to Paula, Robert, Wendy, Paul, Jimmy, Rebecca, Mike and many other friends for their contributions.

Foreword

What is the appeal of Jewish humour? In today's world of multi-racial communities, it's the humour of ethnic minorities. Because Jews have been in a minority in many lands for a couple of millennia they have built up the ultimate ethnic minority humour. It's a humour that's full of received slights and insults (imagined and real); anguish about identity – the fear of losing it and the wish to lose it and merge into the larger social mass; jokes about the impossibility of assimilation; sexual innocence; making light of disastrous circumstances. These aspects of Jewish humour are shared by other minorities – indeed the British Indian hit comedy series *Goodness Gracious Me*, with its ferocious self-mockery, especially on the subject of assimilation, struck a big chord with Jewish viewers.

Other aspects of Jewish humour such as the stories about perennial characters, mostly from the now vanished world of Yiddish-speaking Eastern Europe, are more specifically Jewish. The schnorrer or Jewish beggar, who is always intolerably arrogant; the rabbi's wife, seldom as holy as her husband; the marriage broker, an utter incompetent who lets the cat out of the bag. Or logic, much beloved by our spiritual fathers, is cruelly mocked in Jewish jokes, by being taken to insane lengths.

There have been many Jewish humorists – particularly in America – but this merely reflects the importance of humour in Jewish life. And I have enlivened the parade of jokes in this book with some funny remarks by some celebrated Jewish wits. Groucho Marx, Woody Allen et al don't necessarily deal in specifically Jewish humour and they don't all tell jokes, indeed they mostly don't. Jackie Mason's routines, which are all about the observation of human behaviour, never contain jokes. But jokes are just mini dramas that can incorporate telling repartee and character observation. And the book of Jewish humour that Sigmund Freud worked on, but never published, was reputedly all about jokes and, of course, about the "Freudian slips" made by marriage brokers.

But I'm over-analysing and forgetting the basics – Jewish humour is like all humour – it's there to make you laugh and I really hope it does. The ethnic dimension is more important than ever – it's vital to oil the wheels of multi-ethnic communities and to defeat the puritanical busybodies who think it's bad for us. Remember, if humour is offensive, it isn't funny and therefore isn't humour, so *ipso facto* there's no such thing as offensive humour.

Now that's Jewish logic!

Although a lot of the jokes in this book also appeared in my two previous books – *The World's Best Jewish Jokes* and *More of the World's Best Jewish Jokes*, published some twenty years ago and long out of print, many of the best in this book are new – to me at least.

Paradoxically, in spite of the fame of Jewish humour, there aren't that many good Jewish jokes – and if you doubt me, check the internet. The best ones are here, but if I've missed any good ones send them to me at the publisher's address and I'll use them in the next edition.

Ben Eliezer 2003

Hetty is astonished to see her husband blowing a kiss to a beautiful woman as she is driven off in a taxi.

"Who was that, Morrie?" she demands.

"My mistress."

Hetty is aghast.

"Your what?"

"I said my mistress and don't complain! You've got a flat in Mayfair, a house in Cannes, a BMW, a gold card, an account at Harrod's – and I've got one mistress."

"OK," she sniffed.

A week later they are at the theatre and they see Joe Goldberg, an old friend, with a young woman, who is definitely not his wife.

"Who's that woman?" hisses Hetty to Morrie.

"That? That's Joe's mistress."

"Hmm. She's not as pretty as our mistress."

***

***

Joe and Hymie are walking one fine day in Brooklyn, New York, when they pass a Catholic Church which sports a big notice on the outside:

CONVERT TODAY AND TAKE HOME $25!

Hymie: "That's a steal! I'm going in."

Joe: "You're disgusting! And if it's a joke it's not even funny."

Hymie: "I'm not joking. I'm going in…"

Joe: "What? Five thousand years of our history, the sufferings of our martyrs, the inquisition, the holocaust – and you just throw it all…"

Hymie: "Relax! Calm down! I'll just pretend. It's for the money. Wait for me, I'll be out in half an hour."

Into the church marches Hymie. A half hour comes and goes. Joe paces nervously outside. Eventually Hymie emerges.

"Well?" Joe cries, shaking him. "Did you get the money?"

Hymie looks at him with distaste and says: "What's the matter with you people? Can't you think about anything but money?"

***

★★★

At a very orthodox Jewish wedding when, of course, men must not dance with women, only with each other and the women must do likewise, the groom, emboldened by a few shots of vodka and enflamed by the sight of his plump, untouched newly wed dancing with her girlfriends, approached the Rabbi.

"Rabbi, saintly and learned as you are, please allow me to dance with my wife! We are married now and…"

"No! Never," interrupted the furious Rabbi. "You can dance with your uncle Simon, your cousins Josh and Sam, but you must not dance with a woman, even if she is your wife!"

Shocked and bewildered by this dogmatic stand, and fearful of what the rules of orthodoxy were going to do to his sex life, and after a few more vodkas, he approached the Rabbi again.

"Rabbi, tell me, on my, er, wedding night, will I be allowed to remove my wife's clothes?"

"Of course!" exclaimed the holy teacher.

"And will we be allowed to make love?"

"Of course! The very first of God's commandments in the Bible says thou shalt be fruitful and multiply!"

"And will I be allowed to get on top of my wife?"

"Of course!"

"And will my wife be allowed to get on top of me?"

"Of course!" exclaimed the Rabbi.

"And are we allowed to make love standing up?"

The Rabbi's enraged fist slammed to the table.

"No! No! No!" he thundered.

"But why, Rabbi, why?"

"It could lead to dancing!"

At the funeral service for a rich Jewish banker, one of the mourners is beating his breast and wailing with much more passion than the others. The rabbi, much concerned, taps him on the shoulder.

"I'm so sorry for you, no doubt you're one of the deceased's close relations?"

"No! No!" sobbed the man. "That's why I'm crying!"

***

★★★

When his son is about to enter his business Joe Levy decides the time has come to give the boy a lesson in business morality. He calls him into his office and says:

"Solly, every businessman needs ethics, he must know what is right and wrong in business as well as in his personal life. Now I'll give you an example: a man comes into the shop and buys something for a pound and he gives me a twenty pound note. I just count him out nine pounds, and he leaves the shop without waiting for the rest. Obviously he thought he'd only given me a tenner. Now, what is the ethical question here?"

Solly scratches his head and says that obviously he must chase after his customer and give him the other ten pounds.

But his father disagrees. "No, no, of course not! The ethical question that arises is: should I tell my partner or not?"

★★★

A Jew, a Mr Green, from London's East End is travelling by night sleeper train to visit his son in Glasgow. He shares his compartment with a non-Jew, Mr Robinson.

As they are preparing for bed, Mr Green says: "Excuse me, I wonder if I could bother you? May I borrow your towel, I seem to have left mine at home?" Robinson lends him his towel. A little later, just as Robinson is falling asleep, Green says, "Do please excuse me but I seem to have forgotten my pyjamas. Could I please borrow your vest, only it's getting quite cold, we must be getting close to Watford already?"

Robinson lends Green his vest. A half hour later Green wakes poor Robinson.

"Excuse me, so sorry to bother you, but I seem to have mislaid, or perhaps forgotten, my toothbrush. Do you think I could borrow yours, also perhaps an inch or two of toothpaste?"

This time the long-suffering Robinson has had enough.

"No! No! No! Leave me alone – I have a meeting in the morning, I'm getting no sleep and I share my toothbrush with nobody. It's disgusting!"

The next morning the young Mr Green meets his father at Glasgow's Central Station.

"Well, Dad, how was the trip?"

"OK, but I was sharing with such an anti-semite!"

***

***

Arthur Miller took Marilyn Monroe to her first Jewish restaurant. He ordered chicken soup with matzo balls. She called to the waiter and whispered in his ear: "Hey, do you think I could have another part of the animal?"

***

During an air-raid warning in Tel Aviv when Iraqi bombers and scud missiles were heading that way, two Israelis were rushing for the shelters.

"Oy!" shouted old Benny. "I've left my dentures behind!"

"So?" said Morrie. "What do you think they're dropping? Sandwiches?"

Two Jewish mothers meet while out shopping.

"Well, Ruthie, how are the kids?"

"To tell you the truth, my Abie has married a slut. She doesn't get out of bed until 11, she's out all day spending his money on God knows what, and when he gets home, exhausted from work at the hospital, does she have a good dinner there waiting for him? Psha! She makes him take her out to dinner to an expensive restaurant!"

"And how's the daughter, Esther?"

"Ah! Esther has married a saint. He brings her breakfast in bed, he's given her a gold card so she can buy anything she needs, and in the evening he takes her out to dinner at a smart restaurant!"

★★★

***

Two Jews meet on a train. The younger one asks the elder one the time.

No answer. Again he asks, this time in a louder voice. Again, no answer. Eventually he taps the man on the knee and almost shouts his question.

At last, reluctantly, the elder Jew tells him the time.

"And why did this process take so long, may I ask?" enquires the younger man.

"Well, it's like this. When we get to Minsk you won't know anyone, so I'll ask you home for dinner with my family. I have a beautiful young daughter, you'll fall in love with her, and you're a nice looking boy, no problem. But do I want a son-in-law who doesn't even own a watch?"

★★★

A young girl is found murdered in a forest in Russia. The local Jewish community is terrified, in full knowledge that Jews would get the blame. Then the Rabbi called a meeting of the local council and announced "Good news! They've just discovered that the girl was Jewish."

★★★

A Jew was having a drink at a hotel bar in the Far East when an oriental gentleman accidentally knocks his Bloody Mary all over his shirt front.

"Hell!" yells the Jew. "You Japanese! First we get Pearl Harbour and now this!"

"Hey, hold on! I'm Chinese, not Japanese."

"So? What's in a name?"

"And what about you Jews?" asked the Chinese. "You sank the *Titanic*!"

"We sank what? The *Titanic* was sunk by an iceberg!"

"Iceberg, Goldberg. What's in a name?"

★★★

Woody Allen

Show business is worse than dog eat dog – it's dog doesn't return other dog's phone call.

I sold the story of my love life to a publisher – they're going to make a board game out of it.

The food in that restaurant is terrible – and such small portions.

I don't want to achieve immortality through my films – I want to achieve it by not dying.

I will not eat oysters. I want my food dead. Not sick, not wounded. Dead.

Death is a wonderful way to cut down on expenses.

I got this watch from my grandfather. He sold it to me on his deathbed.

A Catholic priest, an Anglican vicar and a Rabbi were discussing how they divided up the money they collected between the poor of the parish, which they all called God's share, and what they kept for their own subsistence.

The priest said, "I draw a circle on the ground, throw the money in the air and whatever lands in the circle is for the poor, the rest I keep for my own humble needs."

The vicar said, "I draw a square on the ground, throw the money in the air and whatever lands in the square is mine, for my modest requirements, the rest is God's share, for the poor."

The Rabbi said, "Well, it's simple, I just throw it all in the air and what God wants he keeps, anything he lets fall to the ground I keep."

***

***

Adolf Hitler was so infuriated by the flood of anti-Nazi jokes that became popular after he came to power that he ordered the Gestapo to find the man responsible and to bring him before him. The Gestapo, after much research, arrested the Jewish comedian Yossel von Goldbloom and dragged him into the Führer's presence.

"Did you invent the one about me and the ass?" Hitler roared at him.

"Yes, I'm afraid so," admitted von Goldbloom.

"And what about that ridiculous slander that I have only one ball?" he demanded.

"Yes, that was me too," muttered the comedian.

"What about the one that says the day I die will be a Jewish holiday?"

"That one too, I'm afraid," muttered the comic.

"You pig of a Jew!" screamed Hitler. "Don't you realize I'm the Führer of the Third Reich – a great empire that will last a thousand years!"

"Ha! Ha!" shrieked von Goldbloom. "That's hilarious, but you can't blame me for that! I haven't heard it before."

***

Groucho Marx

Don't put any ice in my drink – it takes up too much room.

Tell the florist to send two dozen roses to Mrs Upjohn and write "Emily, I love you" on the back of the bill.

These are my principles – but if you don't like them I have others.

Yes, I can see you bending over a hot stove – I just can't see the stove.

My sex life is now reduced to a fan letter from an elderly lesbian wanting to borrow $800.

Marry me, and I swear I'll never look at another horse.

Will you marry me? How much money have you got? Answer the second question first!

***

A very orthodox former Talmud scholar returns home to Vilna after years in America.

"Tell me," says his mother, shocked by his appearance. "What happened to your beard?"

"No one wears beards in Los Angeles, Mama, I shaved it off."

"Do you still go to synagogue every day?" she pressed.

"That's quite impossible in America, Mama, there are meetings, seminars, think tanks, brainstorms. You can't miss them or you don't get ahead."

"Well, you go on Sabbath at least!"

"Mama, people work Saturdays in America."

"Did you go on Yom Kippur at least?"

"I would have done but I was out of town that day – but I did skip lunch."

"Tell me, are you still circumcised?"

★★★

A schnorrer (a Jewish beggar) called on Mrs Finklestein who took pity on him.

"Here, my man, you may have this. Eat it and be well and may the light of the Lord shine upon you." And she gave him a delicious hunk of chollah (white bread).

Next day he came back for some more, and with some reluctance, Mrs Finklestein gave him more.

The day after that he returned again, only to be given a lump of coarse black bread.

"What?" he exclaimed. "No more chollah?"

"Certainly not," responded Mrs Finklestein. "Chollah is much more expensive."

"Lady, lady," replied the beggar. "Believe me, it's worth it."

★★★

***

Two old Jews met in the street. Yossel stammers and Mendel limps.

"M-m-m-endel," says Yossel, "l-l-l-isten to m-m-my idea how to stop l-l-l-imping."

"Yes, well?"

"Walk with one f-f-foot on the p-p-pavement and one f-f-foot in the g-g-gutter."

"I see, and I've got a method to stop stammering."

"W-w-w-what is it?" asks Yossel excitedly.

"Keep your stupid mouth shut."

***

The same Yossel met another acquaintance in the street.

"So, Yossel, how are you doing?" he was asked.

"N-n-n-not so g-g-good. I ap-p-plied for a j-j-job and the b-b-b-loody antisemites turned me down."

"Poor you, what was the job?"

"A n-n-news read-d-der on rad-d-dio."

***

***

Three Jewish mothers are boasting about how much their sons love them and their fabulous generosity towards them. The first says: "My son bought me a round-the-world cruise ticket, First Class – I'll be away six months!"

The second says: "Bah! That's nothing, my son has chartered a jet to take me and all my friends away to celebrate my birthday in a fabulous resort on the other side of the world!"

The third says: "Rubbish! Listen to this! Twice a week my son goes to the top psychiatrist in New York, at $300 a time and lies on a couch and all they do is talk. And you know what they talk about? Me!"

***

A schnorrer (a Jewish beggar) managed to get to see Lord Rothschild.

"My Lord," he announced. "I have a foolproof way for you to make half a million pounds."

"And how is that?"

"Well, I hear that when your daughter marries you'll give her a dowry of a million pounds."

"That's correct."

"OK – I'll marry her for half a million!"

******

A schnorrer (a Jewish beggar) approaches Lord Rothschild in the street and holds out his cap for alms. Rothschild lifts his hand and says he's very sorry but does not discuss money matters in the street.

The beggar is outraged. "What do you want me to do – open an office?"

***

Sam Cohen is in serious trouble. His business is nearly bankrupt, his partner has run off with the little money left in the bank, his children don't work and he owes a fortune to the moneylender. Eventually things get so bad he goes to the synagogue and prostrates himself before the altar. "Please, God! Please let me win the lottery." But things get worse, his wife leaves him and his creditors are threatening him with bankruptcy. Again he goes to the synagogue, prostrates himself before the altar, tears his clothes, bangs his head on the floor and entreats the Lord on high to let him win the lottery. To no avail. His house is repossessed, he sleeps on the poorhouse floor, the bankruptcy hearing is scheduled for Tuesday. Again he goes to the synagogue, prostrates himself before the altar, tears his clothes, pulls out half his beard and begs the good lord to help him win the lottery.

Suddenly there's a terrifying roaring noise and a clap of thunder and the voice of the Lord echoes through the synagogue. "Sam! Sam!" the great deep voice intones "For goodness' sake, meet me halfway. At least buy a lottery ticket."

***

★★★

Mrs Cohen arrives at Mrs Levy's house for a morning cup of coffee.

"Mmm!" she enthuses. "What a wonderful scent, where do you get such beautiful flowers?"

"Ech, it's nothing. I get a bouquet like that every day of the year."

"So who sends it to you? Do you have a lover?"

"You're crazy! My husband gives them to me."

"Your husband? And what do you have to do for them?"

"Do for them? I have to spend my life on my back with my legs in the air!"

"Why? You've got no vase?"

★★★

The teacher asked Solly, who was at the back of the class: "Tell me Solly, what's three per cent?" Solly shrugged and replied: "You're right, what's three per cent?"

***

Old Abie Cohen is on his death bed. He calls his beloved wife to him and she sits by him and takes his hand.

"Hetty! I'm going!"

"Don't leave me!"

"Hetty, before I go I want to be sure the business is left to my Sammy, the eldest."

"Nonsense," says Hetty. "Not Sammy, he's only interested in enjoying himself, leave it to young Izzy, he's serious."

"OK, and the beach house I want to leave to Naomi..."

"Psha, she hates the sea, leave it to Ruthie!"

"OK, the jewellery I'll leave to Naomi!"

"Nonsense!" says Hetty. "She's a scruff, leave it to Sarah!"

"OK, the car I'll leave to Sammy."

"No! No! He can hardly drive, leave it to Jake."

Abie raises his head with a final effort, and croaks:

"Hetty, can I ask you something?"

"Sure, Abie, go ahead."

"Tell me, who's dying?"

***

Henny Youngman

I told my father I got punished by my teacher for not knowing where the Azores were. He told me to remember where I put things in future.

I buy life insurance year after year – but I haven't been lucky yet.

This time of year always makes me feel sad. Exactly ten years ago I lost my wife. That was some poker game.

It was so cold last winter I saw a lawyer put his hands in his own pockets.

My wife's a light eater – as soon as it gets light she starts eating.

***

Sitting next to well-known socialite Ruthie Plotnek at a gala ball, an admirer, noticing the enormous diamond in the ring on her finger, cannot restrain himself from expressing his admiration for it.

"Sure," she replied. "It's famous, it's fantastic, it's the Plotnek diamond."

"It's incredible," says her admirer. "Tell me about it."

"The Plotnek diamond came from Nepal, it's a blue cabachon stone of one-hundred-and-fifty carats. But it has a curse on it."

"My word!" exclaims her admirer. "What curse?"

"Mr Plotnek!"

***

★★★

Yossel Levy had been saving up all his life to go on a cruise when he retired.

His wife accompanied him to the port and waved him goodbye as he passed through passport control, all set for a cruise of the Caribbean Sea. He toiled up the gangplank with his luggage, dreaming of a cool glass of champagne with the captain and, who knows, maybe a shipboard romance…

But the second he entered the ship, rough hands grabbed him, stripped off his clothes and thrust him down stinking, rotten stairs into a huge cavernous area in the belly of the ship. The light was dim and the air was fetid. Amid harsh confusing shouts he was shackled to a plank and a huge rough oar was thrust into his hands. Then came the frightening sound of drums and a huge bald man came in down the centre gangway beating drums to a heavy uniform rhythm. "Row you scum, row!" he shouted and every so often he waved a fierce whip at the oarsmen.

Next to Yossel on the bench was a white-haired skeleton of a man who could barely lift his oar. All the time the huge man beat the drums or waved his whip and Yossel tried desperately to row in time.

Day after day and night after night this continued until they reached Jamaica.

But Yossel and the other oarsmen did not get out. Instead they had to row all the way back to New York harbour.

Eventually after many more days and nights of exhausting rowing to the crack of the whip and the beat of the drum they arrived back in New York.

As they tied up, Yossel turned to the old man next to him and whispered, "Tell me, I've never been on a cruise before, how much should I tip the drummer?"

The old man shrugged and answered in a hoarse croak:

"Well, I don't really know but when I did the same cruise last year I gave him $10."

***

A Jew owns a remarkable parrot that can pray in Hebrew.

He decides, after making it practise day in and day out for a month to take it down to the synagogue hall at a reception he was invited to, and make some money. After the reception he gathers some twenty acquaintances round him. "This parrot can pray," he announced. "He knows all the Psalms by heart."

Odds of 25 to 1 against are agreed and all his friends put down some money on the table.

"OK, go ahead," he instructs the parrot. Nothing.

The parrot doesn't move or say a word.

"Go on, pray!" he yells. To no avail. He has to pay out a fortune to his snickering friends. He takes the parrot home and is about to strangle it when the parrot says:

"Wait! Wait, you idiot. See what odds you get next week!"

***

At a resort in the Catskill mountains where Jewish ladies go in desperate search for husbands two of them are sitting at the bar commiserating with each other when a nice looking man comes in. One of the ladies button-holes him immediately

"Hi, there! I haven't seen you around here before, where have you been?"

"Well, lady I've been away...at school."

"So, and what have you been studying, medicine?"

"No, actually I've...been in the can."

"The can? What's a can?"

"Prison. I've been in prison for thirty years."

"Oh, wow! What did you do? Steal a lot of money?"

"No, lady. I killed my wife. I chopped her into a lot of small pieces."

"So! You're single!"

***

***

The old man is dying upstairs and the whole household is preparing for the inevitable. His wife especially is busy making chopped liver, bagels with smoked salmon and cream cheese and so on. Soon the tantalising smell of the chopped liver, his favourite dish, reaches the nostrils of the dying man. He calls out for his son.

"Solly," he croaks, "go down and ask your mother to let me have a little bit of the liver on a small piece of white bread. Go, go!"

Five minutes later the son comes back up into his father's bedroom.

"Well?" whispers the old man. "Where is it? Bring it here."

Solly shuffles his feet uncomfortably.

"I'm sorry Dad, but Mum wouldn't let me have any."

"Why? Why?" croaks the incredulous old man.

"She says it's for after."

***

***

A Jewish farmer met an old friend, also a farmer, in the main street of their local market town in Galicia, Eastern Poland.

"So, how's things?"

"Wonderful, especially since I got this new horse that I put to the plough."

"How so? What's this horse got that's so special?"

"I'm teaching it to do with much less food, and he doesn't mind. On the contrary he looks better and he works better. I just feed him every other day, instead of every day."

A fortnight later the two meet again, in the same market town.

"So how's things. How's the wonder horse?"

"Fantastic! I fed him only once every three days for a time and for the last week I only fed him once every four days. He's working better than ever!"

A week later they met again and after the usual query about the wonder horse, the old farmer threw his hat to the ground in disgust.

"That damned, God-forsaken animal! I'd just taught him how to do without food entirely and what does the stupid animal do? He drops dead!"

***

While on his pastoral rounds Father O' Brien sees two small children playing in the road. He recognises one of them, Michael Murphy, as one of his flock. "Well, boys, there's a dollar to whoever can tell me the name of the greatest man who ever lived."

Michael immediately answers: "President John Kennedy!"

"No, no, Michael," says the priest. "You can do better than that." Michael thought and said, "St. Patrick, he brought Christianity to Ireland."

"No, Michael, it's a good answer but it's not the right one."

Then the other little boy spoke. "I know! I know!" he said.

"Oh, and what's your name?"

"Izzy Goldstein," the boy said to the priest. "And the greatest man was Jesus Christ."

"But surely a boy of your faith doesn't think that?" said the puzzled priest, giving him the dollar.

"No," replied Izzy. "But business is business."

***

★★★

"Oy, vey! Rabbi Levy, it's a terrible business. Old Evie Ginsberg owes the money lender $500 and she hasn't got two beans. The money lender must be paid or they'll throw her out of her apartment. She can't work with her bad back, she can barely feed her children, it's a catastrophe!"

"Terrible," agrees the Rabbi. "I'll find some money from the synagogue welfare fund and get some help from a couple of our richer members, we'll find the money somehow. And what's your involvement, are you a relation?"

"Me? Nah, I'm the money lender."

★★★

Molly Levy takes her little grandson to the beach and immediately starts the warnings:

"Don't go in the sun – you'll get skin cancer!

"Don't go in the sea – you'll drown!

"Don't go near the sand – you'll get it in your eyes!" When she takes the boy back to his parents she exclaims: "Lovely boy! But so nervous!"

★★★

★★★

Beckie says to Ruthie: "You look so good! Your hair's shiny, your skin's glowing, what's your secret?"

"Well," replies Ruthie, "this is what happened. Last Monday a handsome young man came to the door asking for my Joe: 'Madam,' he said, 'is your husband Joe at home?' When I said no, the young man, strong like a lion, picks me up takes me upstairs, throws me on the bed and makes love to me for an hour. Next day, Tuesday, same time, a knock on the door, same young man, same question, same reply and again he takes me upstairs to the bedroom and makes love to me for three hours. Yesterday, the same thing – this time I'm on the bed with him for four hours. This morning, a knock on the door, same young man, takes me upstairs and makes love to me for five hours. Only one thing puzzles me…"

"What's that?" asks Beckie, who's been listening wide-eyed.

"What does he want with my Joe?"

***

Old Louis Cohen is dead and his wife rings up the *Jewish Chronicle* to put a death announcement in the classified advertising.

"You have our condolences, Madam. And may I personally wish you a long life?" says the advertising manager. "What form would you like the announcement to take?"

"What do you mean?"

"Well, what words do you want to appear?"

"Louis Cohen is dead."

"Is that all? No dates, no details of the children, no religious wishes?"

"No," the old lady replied.

"I understand, but you know the minimum charge is £10 for seven words – you can have three more words free."

"OK then, add 'Volvo for Sale'."

***

A schnorrer (a Jewish beggar) knocks loudly on the front door of the house of a rich Jew at two o'clock in the morning. No answer. He knocks again, very loudly.

The owner of the house wakes up and comes down in a rage to see who dares disturb his household at such an hour. He is astonished to see the beggar there.

"Can I have ten pence, please?" asks the schnorrer.

"What do you think you're doing waking me up in the middle of the night just for ten pence!" rages the rich man

"Listen," replies the beggar, "do me a favour. I don't tell you how to run your business, don't you tell me how to run mine!"

★★★

***

Joe and Esther Goldberg went on a skiing holiday to Switzerland. On the first day Joe told his wife he was going off skiing all day in the high mountains and he wouldn't be back till dusk. She waited nervously all day and when he hadn't returned by eight o'clock at night she begged for a search party to be sent out.

Eventually a Red Cross rescue team – a full complement of guides and St Bernard dogs and army mountaineers – set off for the high slopes. They called as they went: "Mr Goldberg! Mr Goldberg! It's the Red Cross! Where are you?"

No reply. They went higher and higher, calling: "Mr Goldberg! It's the Red Cross." Still no reply, not a sign of life. Eventually they are nearly at the glacier and they call out again:

"Mr Goldberg! Mr Goldberg! It's the Red Cross!"

This time a faint answer comes back: "I've given already!"

Two partners have been in the rag trade all their lives but times have got so hard and the older one, Bennie, is so depressed that he decides to end it all and leap from the window of their 52nd floor showroom at the heart of New York's fashion district. Bennie shakes hands with Jack one last time and leaps from the window. As he sails past the window of a competitor on the 24th floor he yells back up: "Jack! Lace cuffs next season!"

★★★

Two Jews are in front of a firing squad. They are offered a blindfold. One refuses it with a curse. The other whispers: "Shh! Don't make trouble!"

★★★

An old Jew is run over by a truck in front of a church. Hearing the commotion a priest runs out from the church to tend to the badly injured man. The priest whispers to him: "Do you believe in the Father, the Son and the Holy Ghost?"

The old Jew opens his eyes and says: "I'm dying and he asks me riddles!"

★★★

A Jewish dilemma - pork sausages at half price.

★★★

What is the explanation for the tradition that, at his marriage, a Jew breaks a glass by treading on it?

It's the last time he gets to put his foot down.

★★★

***

President Bill Clinton was riding in a motorcade over Brooklyn Bridge in New York.

"Jerry," he says to one of his aides. "Why don't we stop somewheres for a nice kosher pastrami sandwich on rye bread?"

"Mr President," replies Jerry. "It so happens I know just the place right here in Brooklyn, Joe Cohen's, near where I was brought up. The motorcade speeds off in a screech of tyres, Secret Service motorcyclists surround the President's car, and draws up in front of a sleepy little sandwich bar. Business was slow and Joe Cohen was mopping down the counter with an old rag, but when he looked up and saw the array of black Cadillacs and outriders heading straight for his shop he couldn't believe his eyes. And when the President himself came in, flanked by aides, he nearly passed out.

"Your Highness! Your Majesty!" he blurted out. "Vot can I do for you?"

"Two dozen pastrami sandwiches on rye, plenty of mustard, to go," said the President.

Joe slaved away, praying that one of his regulars would come by and see the President in his shop – what a boost that would be for his business! But no one came in.

"What do I owe you, Mr ... er ... er ... Cohen?"

"Owe me, Your Highness? Nutting, nutting at all. Vas a great pleasure and an honour."

"That's very kind of you but I must do something!"

"Vell, yes, you could. Come back here same time next week."

At the same time the following week the great motorcade drew up outside Joe Cohen's sandwich bar. This time the scene inside was very different. The place was jammed, people were crawling on top of each other, contorted faces pressed up against the window and all the while Joe and his family were slicing meat, slapping on mustard, making sandwiches like there was no tomorrow and taking in lots of money. As the President forced his way through the crowd a hush fell on the gathering.

"Well, Joe, I'm here," said President Clinton.

"Bill! Bill!" said Joe. "Nice to see you, but not when there's business!"

***

An old Jewish lady was on a train and every few minutes she moaned:

"Oy! Am I thirsty!"

A minute or so later:

"Oy vey, am I thirsty!"

Eventually a smart young man got so irritated by her incessant moaning that he went to the restaurant car and got her a glass of water and thrust it in her hand and sat down again.

She drank the glass gratefully and a minute later said:

"Oy! Was I thirsty! Oy vey! Was I thirsty!"

***

A beggar stops an old lady in the street.

"Madam, have mercy, I'm weak from hunger, I haven't eaten in four days!"

"So?" she says. "Force yourself."

***

Three men were boasting about the sexual passion they could arouse in their wives. Giovanni, an Italian said:

"Last night I covered my wife from head to toe in finest olive oil, massaged her tenderly for an hour, then we made passionate love and she screamed for five minutes!"

Then Pierre, a Frenchman said:
"I covered my wife completely in best Normandy butter, massaged her for an hour with great skill, we made passionate love and at the end she shrieked in ecstasy for a quarter of an hour!"

Then Joe, a Jewish guy spoke:

"Yesterday afternoon I covered my wife in best kosher margarine with a little cold chicken soup, she was completely naked, and I massaged her for an hour and a half. Afterwards we made love for an hour and at the end she screamed for six hours!"

"Six hours!!" cried the other two in astonishment. "How did you do that?"

Joe shrugged: "I wiped my hands on the curtains."

***

***

What is the difference between an Italian mother and a Jewish mother?

An Italian mother says to her son: "Eat your dinner or I'll kill you!"

A Jewish mother says: "Eat your dinner or I'll kill myself!"

***

Solly has been tossing and turning half the night, unable to sleep. Eventually Beckie turns the light on and asks him what is wrong.

"It's that $500 I owe Benny. I promised to repay him tomorrow and I haven't got it."

Beckie opens the window and shrieks across the way:

"Benny! Benny! Solly owes you $500 right? Well he hasn't got it yet and can't repay you tomorrow."

She shuts the window and says to Solly: "Now let Benny do the worrying, you go to sleep!"

It's Abie and Rachel's 20th wedding anniversary and as they're driving to a nice restaurant to celebrate Rachel tells Abie to take the second left and third right, not at all the way they were going.

"Why are we going so out of the way, my sweet nightingale?" he asks.

"You'll see, my sweetest flower. There, look, you see that big new building over the way, it's yours, here are the deeds."

"Rachel! That whole building! It's impossible. How did you do it? Were you left money? How did you pay for it?"

"Abie, you know you've always given me $20 every time we make love? Well, I've saved it and invested it."

"My God!" exclaims a stunned Abie. "If only I'd known I'd have given you all my business."

★★★

Joan Rivers

I hate housework! You make the beds, you do the dishes – and six months later you've got to do it all over again.

A woman went to a plastic surgeon and asked him to make her like Bo Derek. He gave her a lobotomy.

Her legs were apart so often they were pen pals.

Diana Ross is so thin that when she walked into a pool hall they chalked her head.

My acne was so bad that blind people tried to read my face.

I told my mother-in-law that my house was her house and she said to get the hell off her property.

Men don't get cellulite – therefore God might just be a man after all.

When I was little I got a boy to play doctors with me, but he sent me a bill.

Yes I do have flabby thighs but thank goodness my stomach covers them.

You go to a psychiatrist when you're a little cracked and you stop when you're completely broke.

Bo Derek does not understand the concept of Roman numerals. She thought we fought in World War Eleven.

***

At a Jewish restaurant a regular customer is astonished to be served by a Chinese waiter who speaks fluent Yiddish. After dinner he spoke to the owner:

"Tell me, how come you've got a Chinese waiter who speaks Yiddish?"

"Sshh!" replied the owner. "He thinks it's English."

***

An old Jew is run over by a car. He is laid gently by the side of the road. Someone fetches a blanket and a cushion from a nearby shop. A woman wraps him up and puts the cushion under his head.

"Tell me, are you comfortable?" she asks. The old man thinks for a moment and says "Well, I make a living."

***

Mrs Ginsberg has two female parrots and she is so horrified by their behaviour she consults the Rabbi about them.

"Rabbi, my parrots are a disgrace, I don't know what to do. They sit in their cage fluffing up their feathers and prancing about and saying in the loudest voices as soon as anyone comes near: 'Hi, everyone, we're a couple of good time girls, anyone for sex?' Can you believe it? What can I do?"

The Rabbi was much less alarmed than she expected.

"Don't worry Mrs Ginsberg," he reassured her. "The most devout and learned member of the congregation, Isaac Levy, has two male parrots which are the epitome of holiness. They pray all day long, swaying to and fro on their perches just like students at a Talmud Torah (a religious school). If you take your two naughty parrots and place them near the good parrots of Mr Levy, a miracle will happen and they too will become devout. I promise you."

Mrs Ginsberg was much comforted by the Rabbi's promises and took her two wicked fowl along to Mr Levy's house. Mr Levy showed her in to his sitting room, where two male parrots were perched and praying for all they were worth in the dim light.

Without further ado they took the two female parrots and placed them in the males' cage. As soon as they were in, true to form, they screeched:

"Hi, everyone, we're a couple of good time girls and we love sex. Anyone interested?"

The two male parrots lifted their prayer shawls in disbelief and one said to the other, tearing off his shawl and throwing his prayer book aside:

"Our prayers are answered! Hi, girls, what kept you?"

A beautiful woman consults Dr Greenburg. He tells her to strip naked and lie on the couch. He lies next to her and makes love to her.

"Well," he said. "That sorts out my problems. Now let's talk about yours."

***

***

A teenage student at a Yeshiva, a religious college, tells his father:

"Dad, I get these terrible urges all the time, what can I do?"

"Go and see your Rabbi, he'll know all about it."

The boy goes to the rabbi and explains:

"Even in the middle of a lesson I get erections."

"Pray harder," says the Rabbi.

"Well?" asks his father when he returns home.

"He said pray harder, but I pray as hard as I can already."

He returned to the Rabbi for further advice but the Rabbi was out and, on her insistence, explains the problem to the Rabbi's wife. She takes him upstairs to the bedroom and makes love to him.

"Well, what did he say this time?" asked his father on his return.

"Nothing, he was out. But I'll tell you, the rabbi's wife has more brains between her legs than the rabbi has in his head!"

***

When Groucho Marx was told he couldn't swim in the pool of the country club he was visiting, because of his race, he asked the official if his son, who was only half Jewish could go in up to his waist.

Groucho also famously observed that he'd never want to join any club that would accept him.

***

A group of Jewish women who met regularly for coffee decided that they were finished with talking about their hairdressers, their children, their sons-in-law or their au pairs and that henceforth they would only talk about intellectual topics such as books and politics. When, early on in the new style conversations, Hanna asked:

"And what do we all think about Red China?" Sarah answered immediately:

"Wonderful. Especially on a white table cloth."

★★★

The Emperor of Japan is seeking an ace Samurai, the best in Japan, to become the head of the Imperial Bodyguard. After many interviews and trials of strength and skill in the ancient martial arts, the candidates are reduced to a short list of three: a Japanese Samurai, a Chinese Samurai and a Jewish Samurai.

It's time for the final interviews and the Japanese goes in first.

He bows low as a fly is released into the room from a matchbox and buzzes around noisily. The Samurai draws his sword, waves it above his head, shouts a war cry and after a single whoosh the fly drops dead at the Emperor's feet, neatly sliced in two.

"Very impressive," murmurs the Emperor.

Then the Chinese samurai enters, bows to the ground as another fly is released into the room. With a tremendous cry the samurai draws his sword and with a whoosh and another whoosh the fly instantly stops buzzing and falls at the Emperor's feet, neatly sliced in four equal pieces.

"Most impressive," says the Emperor.

Then the Jewish samurai enters and exactly the same ritual occurs. But this time the samurai makes a whoosh and another whoosh and a third whoosh but the fly continues buzzing round the room.

"Hmm," murmurs the Emperor. "After all that, the fly still seems in excellent shape."

"Ah so," said the Jewish samurai, bowing low. "But it is in our tradition that circumcision should do the patient no harm."

★★★

A Catholic priest, an Anglican vicar and a rabbi are discussing their own funerals.

"What," asked the priest, "would you like to have the leader of your congregation say over your coffin?"

"Well," answered the vicar, "I'd like to hear someone say that I played a straight bat in the game of life, that I bowled an honest ball and was a brave team leader. What about you, Father?"

"I would like it to be said that I was a saintly and comforting shepherd to my flock. What about you, rabbi?"

"Me? Over my coffin? I'd like to hear someone shout: 'Look! He's moving!'"

★★★

Rita Rudner

The best place to meet men is the dry cleaners – at least you know they have a job and bathe.

To attract men I wear a perfume called New Car Interior.

Women will sometimes at least admit to making a mistake. The last man to admit to making a mistake was General Custer.

Men with pierced ears will make the best husbands – they're accustomed to pain and have bought jewellery.

Three wise men? Is that a joke?

My grandmother was a very tough woman – she buried three husbands and two of them were just napping.

If your husband finds it hard to fall asleep, the words "we need to discuss our relationship" should help.

An old Jew who fancied he still enjoyed the virility of youth went to a sperm bank and offered his services. The nurse gave him a bottle and showed him to a curtained cubicle.

"When you've finished please refasten the bottle, write your name on the label and leave it on my desk."

The old man went into the cubicle and the nurse went to have a cup of tea. About a quarter of an hour later she returned expecting to see the sealed bottle on her desk. Instead she heard heavy breathing from the cubicle. She went over to it and asked:

"Mr Cohen, are you all right?"

More groaning noises.

"Mr Cohen can you manage all right? Would you prefer to come back another day?"

"Nah," came the reply from the cubicle, "it's … just … that … I … can't take … the top off … the bottle!"

***

★★★

An old Jew was ill of a rare disease and the only treatment that the doctors thought could help was a regular supply of milk. A local nurse who had just had a baby and who had a plentiful supply of breast milk was hired to treat the old man. He lapped away contentedly at her breast for a quarter of an hour and, indeed, started to feel better. At the next session two days later he's again lapping away at the nurse's ripe breast when, in spite of herself, the nurse starts to become aroused.

"Tell me, Mr Levy, is there perhaps anything else you'd like?"

"You know something nurse? I would like something else."

"What?" she breathed huskily.

"Maybe, just a little biscuit?"

★★★

***

A rabbi finds he is sharing a rail compartment with a Roman Catholic priest. After some moments of idle chatter, the priest leans forward. "Excuse me, rabbi, but is it true that men of your faith may not eat pork?"

"Yes, Father, that is true," answered the rabbi.

"That's a shame – it can be really delicious. Tell me, Rabbi, have you ever tasted it?"

"Well, yes," answered the rabbi. "To be honest, I did once eat half a pork chop without knowing."

"And what did you think, rabbi, was it good?"

"Yes, actually, it tasted rather good."

A little later the rabbi leant forward and asked:

"Tell me, Father, is it true that men of the cloth in your religion may not have sexual intercourse with women?"

"Yes," replied the priest, "that is true."

"And tell me Father, have you ever tried it?"

"Well, no, rabbi, as it happens, I haven't."

"Hmmm, pity," says the rabbi. "It's better than pork."

★★★

Father O'Malley, parish priest of the church of
St Saviour in Golders Green, North London,
calls on his good friend Rabbi Goldbloom of
the Hampstead Garden Suburb synagogue, in a
state of considerable agitation.

"Rabbi, rabbi, you've got to help me. I've
confession starting in ten minutes and I have to
be away at a funeral in Hendon in three quarters
of an hour. Will you stand in for me? Only for
an hour, but Father Murphy's off sick, and I've
no one else to turn to."

"What, me? Take confession? I don't know the
first thing…"

"It's a piece of cake, and only for an hour when
I'll be back and maybe no one will come in.
Come down to the church now and hide near
me, I'll start off and you'll get the hang of it in no
time at all."

They got to the church and the priest sat in
the confessional while the rabbi sat in a hidden
area just outside. A woman came in.

"Father, I have sinned," she said.

"What have you done, my child?" asked the
priest.

"I have committed adultery."

"How many times?"

"Four times, Father, and I sincerely repent."

"Put £2 in the box, say ten Hail Marys, repent sincerely and you will be absolved."

Another woman came in.

"Father, I have committed a great sin," she said.

"And what have you done, my child?" asked the priest, looking at his watch.

"I made love to the lodger."

"How many times?"

"Twice, and I'll never do it again."

"Put £1 in the box, say five Hail Marys and you'll be absolved."

When the woman had left, the priest said to the rabbi, "OK, got it? You take over now, I'll be back as soon as I can." And he dashed off to the funeral.

The rabbi climbed into the confessional and waited.

Soon a woman came in.

"Father, I have sinned most grievously," she said.

"What have you done, my child?" asked the rabbi.

"I have committed a sin of the flesh. I have fornicated."

"How many times, my child?"

"Just the once, Father."

"Hmmm," ruminated the rabbi. "You'd better go and do it again."

"What?" cried the woman. "Do it again?"

"Sure, it's two for a quid."

***

In the days of the Soviet Union when a lot of Jews were trying to emigrate to Israel a KGB man came across a Jew reading a book in Hebrew on a bench in Moscow's Gorky Park.

"Hey, Jew," he said. "Don't waste your time, you know we'll never let you go and live in Israel."

"I know that. I'm reading it in case they speak Hebrew in heaven."

"And what happens if you go to hell?" asked the man from the KGB.

"Ah! Russian I already know!"

***

***

What's the difference between a British gentleman and a Jew at a party?

The gentleman leaves but doesn't say goodbye and the Jew says goodbye but doesn't leave.

***

Little Abie had stolen the rabbi's gold watch. He didn't feel too good about it, so he decided, after a sleepless night to go to the rabbi.

"Rabbi, I stole a gold watch."

"Abie! You know that is forbidden! You should return it immediately!"

"What should I do?"

"Why! Give it back to the owner, of course!"

"Do you want it?"

"No, I said return it to its owner."

"But he doesn't want it."

"In that case, you can keep it."

***

★★★

A Jewish town had a shortage of eligible bachelors, so they had to import men from other towns. One day an eligible bachelor arrived on a train, and hopeful mothers-in-law, Mrs Ginsberg and Mrs Goldberg, were waiting for him, each claiming ownership of him.

A local very wise rabbi, who fancied himself as something of a King Solomon, was called to resolve the issue. After deliberating for a few minutes he said:

"Since you both want the groom, I'll have to cut him in half and give each one of you half of him."

Mrs Goldberg remained silent but Mrs Ginsberg immediately said:

"If that's the case, give him to Mrs Goldberg. I couldn't bear to see such a thing."

The rabbi said in judgement: "Give him to Mrs Goldberg. If she's willing to cut him in half she must be the correct mother-in-law."

***

A man walked into the lingerie department of Harrod's. He shyly walked up to the woman behind the counter and said. "I wonder if you can help me, I'd like to buy a brassiere for my wife".

"What type of bra?" asked the sales lady.

"Type?" enquires the man. "There is more than one type?"

"Sure," said the sales lady, and she showed him a pile of bras of every shape, size, colour and fabric. "There are four basic types of bra," said the sales lady. "The Catholic type, the Salvation Army type, the Presbyterian type and the Jewish type. Which one do you need?"

"What is the difference between them?"

"It is all really quite simple. The Catholic type supports the masses, the Salvation Army type lifts up the fallen, the Presbyterian type keeps them staunch and upright and the Jewish type makes mountains out of mole hills."

***

Max Kaufman

We were fast and furious. I was fast and she was furious.

I never knew what happiness was until I got married – but by then it was too late.

My son has taken up meditation. At least it's better than sitting around doing nothing.

In the days of high inflation two friends meet in a Manchester street.

"Well how are?"

"Terrible! I've been very ill. I've been away from work for five months and it's cost me £2000 on medicines and doctors."

"My God, that's terrible. Five years ago you could have been ill for a year on that kind of money!"

***

★★★

A poor Jew says to his wife "Let's have blintzes for a change."

"Don't be foolish, only rich people can afford blintzes."

"Why?"

"Well how could we afford eggs?" asks his wife.

"True – so let's have them without eggs."

"And raisins, can we afford raisins?"

"No, true, so we'll eat them without raisins."

"And cottage cheese," she continues. "We have no cottage cheese."

"OK, so we have them without cottage cheese."

When they'd finished eating the man said:

"You know, I don't see what rich people see in blintzes!"

★★★

One cold winter in Moscow, a rumour went around that a certain butcher's shop would have meat for sale the next day. By very early in the morning, a long queue had formed outside of the shop. But at 8 o'clock a Communist party official came out briefly and announced, "Comrades, I'm afraid there's not enough meat for everybody here. Would all of the Jews leave?"

They did, and the queue was shortened somewhat. At 11 o'clock the official came out again and announced, "Comrades, I'm afraid there's still not enough meat for all. Would all people who are not party members please leave."

They did, and the line was shortened again. At 2 o'clock, the official came out again. "There's still not enough meat for all of you! Would all those who did not defend our great motherland from the fascist invaders please leave."

Once again, the line was considerably shortened. At 8 o'clock in the evening, the official came out again when there were just a few, half-frozen people left in the queue. This time he announced, "There isn't any meat at all. You must all go home."

The old men moved slowly away, grumbling among themselves – and one said to the other, "How come those damned Jews got the best deal?"

***

Three partisans are about to be executed. They are each asked what they would like for their last meal.

The Italian said: "I'll have Pappardelle alla Vongole and a bottle of Barolo red."

The Frenchman said: "Give me Turbot Cardinale with quenelles d'ecrevisses and a bottle of Montrachet."

The Jew said: "I'll have a bowl of strawberries."

"That's impossible," said the captain of the guard. "They're not in season yet."

"So I'll wait!"

***

Golda Meir used to say that Israelis didn't admire Moses. He led us around the desert for forty years and took us to the only part of the whole region that had no oil.

★★★

A rabbi's two disciples arrived at his home one afternoon for a lesson in Talmud.

The maid served them with two cups of tea and two cakes, one big and one small one.

"After you," said the first disciple pointing to the plate with the cakes on it.

"No, no, after you," insisted the second.

"No, no, my friend, after you."

"Absolutely not, no way, you take first please."

"No, no, no, after you I insist, my dear friend."

"No, no, no. You take first, please, my very good friend."

Eventually the first disciple helped himself and took the bigger cake.

The other was horrified. "What? You helped yourself first and took the bigger cake?"

"Sure," he said "and if you'd taken first which one would you have taken?"

"Why, the smaller cake, of course!"

"Well, you've got the smaller cake, so what are you complaining about?"

***

A priest sees the rabbi cross himself as he leaves home one morning.

"Rabbi, wonderful! You've seen the error of your ways. I'm delighted!"

"No, Father, I was just checking I had everything with me: spectacles, testicles, wallet and watch!"

***

How many Jewish mothers does it take to change a light bulb? None.

"Don't worry, I'll sit here in the dark."

How many orthodox Jews? "Change? What's that?"

How many members of a synagogue congregation?

"What, change that light bulb? It was donated by my grandmother!"

***

The church had a plague of mice and so did the synagogue next door. The church warden called in the professional rodent exterminators but within a few weeks the mice were back. The synagogue however did manage to get rid of its mice and the church warden asked the rabbi how they did it. "No problem. We let them in, sat them near the pulpit, gave them a bar mitzvah service (confirmation) and never saw them again!"

Business had been so bad for so long that Joe decided to kill himself so he went to a neighbour's house and gassed himself.

***

★★★

Father McManus of the Church of St Christopher begged Rabbi Levy to teach him the principles of talmudic logic.

"But, Father, you wouldn't understand the spirit behind the Talmud, it's not like the teachings of the church fathers at all."

"Please try me, Rabbi, I'm fascinated by it."

"OK," replied the rabbi, "I'll give you a test. I'll ask you three questions. First: two men come down a chimney. One is clean, the other is all dirty. Which one washes himself?"

"Easy," says the priest. "The dirty one, of course."

"No, it was the clean one because he looked at the dirty one and thought he himself must be just as dirty and so washed himself whereas the dirty man saw the clean man and decided he was clean too so did not wash himself. Get it?"

"Sure thing," said Father McManus. "What's the second question?"

"OK," says the rabbi, "second question: two men come down a chimney, one is dirty, one is clean. Which one washes himself?"

"Why, the clean man, of course."

"No, it's the dirty man because he compares his state to the clean man's so he washes himself.

Third question: two men are coming down a chimney, one's clean the other's dirty. Which one washes himself?"

Father McManus shakes his head in despair, "I no longer know."

"See!" shouts the rabbi. "How could two men come down the same chimney and one be clean and the other dirty?"

Little Sarah swallowed a silver dollar and her mother rushed to the phone to ring the doctor but her husband stopped her.

"Don't waste time with the doctor, ring the synagogue fund raiser, Joe Levy, he can get money out of anybody!"

★★★

★★★

Izzy and Joe have been in business for 25 years and eventually Joe's wife persuades him to take a holiday in Florida. He rings Izzy to find out how business is while he's been away.

"Terrible!" says Izzy. "Thieves broke in last night and stole all the cash, a whole week's takings!"

"Izzy!" said Joe. "Put it back!"

★★★

Ginsberg visits his patient Dr Goldberg, a famous specialist.

"Well," he asks, "what's wrong with me?"

"Nothing, you're fine," replied the great doctor.

"Fine? What about my headaches?"

"I'm not worried about your headaches."

Ginsberg shrugged. "Listen Dr Goldberg, if you had headaches I wouldn't worry about them either!"

★★★

***

Rosenbloom was on his way to Nuremberg market with a duck under his arm. He was stopped in the street by a Nazi brownshirt. "Hey, Jew! Where do you think you are going with that duck?"

"I'm going to the market to buy some food for my duck."

"And what does he eat, your miserable duck?"

"Maize is what he eats."

"Maize? Good Germans are dying of hunger and you Jews are buying maize for your ducks?" He kicked Rosenbloom about and went off.

A little later another Nazi stopped him.

"Where are you off to, Jewish dog?"

"I'm off to the market to get some food for my duck, Sir."

"And what does this scrawny bird of yours eat, Jew?"

"It eats wheat, Sir."

"Wheat?" yelled the Nazi. "Good German soldiers are dying of hunger on the Eastern front and you're buying your duck good wheat?" He slapped Rosenbloom around a bit and went on his way.

Just before he got to the market Rosenbloom was stopped by another Nazi officer.

"Hey, Jewish swine!" he yelled. "Where are you taking that duck?"

"I'm taking it to market to buy it some food."

"And what does he eat, this Jewish duck?"

"I'm not sure," said Rosenbloom. "I'll give it a couple of pfennigs and it can buy what it wants."

***

Dr Goldberg rings Ginsberg in a rage. "That cheque of yours just came back!"

"So did my arthritis."

***

Old Cissie Bloomstein, just retired after a lifetime in the rag trade, is sitting dozing on a bench in the park when a young flasher in a raincoat comes up to her and suddenly opens his raincoat, revealing all. She wakes with a start, looks carefully at the vision before her and shrugs, unimpressed.

"Hmm!" she says. "You call that a lining?"

***

Mort Sahl

In the 1940s to get a girl you had to be a soldier or an airman, in the fifties you had to be Jewish, in the sixties you had to be black. In the seventies to get a girl you had to be a girl.

Ronald Reagan won because he ran against Jimmy Carter. If he had run unopposed he would have lost.

Spiro Agnew's library burned down and both books were destroyed – and one of them hadn't even been coloured in.

Two politicians are drowning and you are allowed to save only one – what do you do? Read your newspaper or eat your lunch?

***

A man rang his psychiatrist, Dr Levy, early one morning insisting on an early appointment. He arrived all out of breath.

"Doctor, doctor, I'm in a terrible state – I had to see you immediately. I had a dreadful dream, what can it mean? It's driving me mad! I dreamt I raped my mother, killed my wife, slept with my daughter and hanged my father. As soon as I woke up I had a quick slice of toast and a cup of coffee and came right over."

Dr Levy gazed at his patient in astonishment.

"What! You call that a breakfast?"

***

What did the Jewish waiter say to a party of Jewish mothers who were dining at his restaurant one evening?

"Good evening ladies, is anything all right?"

★★★

For his 85th birthday Hymie Bloom's friends clubbed together and sent him a very high-class call girl to give him the time of his life. The bell rang at his apartment, he opened the door and there was this beautiful, half-naked girl at his door.

"Hello, Mr Bloom," she cooed. "Happy Birthday! I'm here at the request of your friends to give you super sex!"

"Hmmm," murmured the old man. "I think I'll take the soup."

★★★

Moses arrives at the Red Sea with the Israelites and the Pharaoh's army in hot pursuit. He calls over his spin doctor, Morrie, in a rage. "The boats! Where are the boats?"

"Boats?" asked Morrie. "Who said anything about boats?"

"I must have boats to cross the water, enough boats for the people. What do you want me to do – part the waters and we walk to the other shore?"

"Listen, do that and I'll get you ten whole pages in the Old Testament!"

***

Abe visits his doctor for a routine examination and receives the dreadful news that he is in the last stages of a hideous disease, he's mortally ill, there's no treatment possible and he'll die within a day. He goes back home heartbroken, tells his wife and after they've consoled each other Abe says to his wife, "What say we go to bed and fool around a little since it will be my last night?"

She agreed readily, for a change, and they sleep after making love. At one in the morning Abe wakes her and suggests they have another go. They do and fall asleep.

At three in the morning Abe wakes up and asks his wife again if they can do it once more. This time she's had enough.

"For God's sake Abe, it's easy for you, you don't have to get up in the morning!"

***

Ginsberg goes to Goldfarb's shop to buy a cupboard. "We don't sell furniture any more, we sell clocks. Here, buy a nice clock – I notice you don't wear a wristwatch, so have a clock."

"Na," says Ginsberg. "Who needs a clock? I don't need a clock."

"You don't need a clock? Of course you need a clock, everyone needs a clock. Tell me, wise man, how do you know when to get up in the morning?"

"Easy! The man next door turns his radio on at seven o'clock. I hear the announcer give the time."

"So how do you know when to go to work or when to come home?"

"Easy!" responds Ginsberg. "By the time I get out of bed and have a wash and a shave it's half past seven. By the time I've had a boiled egg and a piece of toast it's a quarter to eight, time to leave for the office. By the time I get to the bus stop it's eight o'clock, the bus comes in a few minutes and by the time it gets to the station it's a quarter past. The train comes at twenty five past and gets me to my office at nine. Which is when I start work. The factory siren next door sounds at twelve o'clock and by the time I've had a walk to buy a paper and eaten my sandwich and chatted about the football results with the boys round the photocopier it's one o'clock. Which is time I get back to work. At five, which is time to leave for home, another siren goes and by the time the train and the bus have taken me home it's six o'clock. By the time I've made something to eat and watched maybe a little television it's time to go to bed. Next morning at seven the neighbour's radio wakes me up and off I go again. So why do I need a clock?"

By this time Goldfarb wishes he'd stayed in the furniture business but he can't resist asking one more question.

"So what happens if you wake up in the middle of the night and want to know what time it is?"

"Easy! I've got a trumpet."

"You've got a trumpet? How do you tell the time with a trumpet?"

"Easy! I go out on the balcony and blow as hard as I can."

"And how does that tell you the time?" asked a desperate Goldfarb.

"Easy! The anti-semite who lives opposite

opens his window and yells: 'Hey, you stupid Jew, what are you doing playing the bloody trumpet at three in the morning!' "

A Jew comes home one night from work and is shocked to be faced with incontrovertible evidence that his wife is being unfaithful to him.

"I'm going to kill her," he tells a friend.

"Don't do that. The police will get you, you'll have a long trial and you'll be sent to a filthy jail for the rest of your life. The best punishment for her would be to screw her to death."

So the Jew makes love to his wife day and night for a year. His friend comes over to visit him and is horrified to find him a haggard, shaking, grey-haired old man. His wife, on the contrary looks wonderful, shining with good health.

"How is it you look so ill and she looks so well?"

"Sshh! Don't say anything – she doesn't know she's dying."

★★★

Jackie Mason

England is the only country in the world where the food is more dangerous than the sex.

I already have enough money to last me the rest of my life – so long as I don't have to buy anything.

Did you hear of the Jewish Santa Claus? He came down the chimney and said to all the children:
"Hi, kids! Do you want to buy some presents?"

★★★

A Jew is sitting on a train opposite a priest.

"Tell me, your er-worship," the Jew says. "Why do you wear your collar back to front?"

"Because I'm a Father."

"I'm also a father," replied the Jew. "And I don't wear my collar like that."

"Ah, but I'm a Father to hundreds."

"Wow! Then maybe you should wear your trousers back to front."

★★★

★★★

Two chauffeurs are waiting by their limousines
for their employers to emerge from evening
prayers at the synagogue. The sound of a ram's
horn trumpet is heard from within.

"Hey, what's that they're doing in there?" asked
one chauffeur to the other.

"They're blowin' the shofar."

"Why, they sure are good to their staff!"

★★★

A very religious rabbi dies and his adoring
followers pray for a glimpse of him in heaven.
They are granted their wish but to their horror
they see him in the clouds with a beautiful, half-
naked girl on his lap.

"Rabbi! Rabbi!" they cry. "How can you
behave like that – you who were always so
saintly?"

"You don't understand," replies the rabbi.
"She's not my reward, I'm her punishment!"

★★★

★★★

Two middle-aged Jews, who were at school together, meet in the street outside London's Savoy hotel. One is expensively dressed and is about to get into a Rolls-Royce, the other is in rags and is a beggar.

"Hey, Nathan, remember me?" cries the beggar. "It's Solly, your old friend. Do me a favour and give me £10 for a bed."

"Sure! Sure," replied Nathan, putting his arm round him. "Bring it round in the morning and I'll take a look at it!"

★★★

A mother gave her son two ties for his birthday: one with blue and white stripes and one with red polka dots on a navy background. To make her happy he wore the polka dotted tie the next time he had dinner with his parents.

When his mother saw him she was horrified and threw her hands in the air.

"What? You don't like the striped tie?"

★★★

★★★

A Jewish man passes by a pet shop and sees a parrot that costs $500. He asks why it costs so much and the salesman tells him the parrot speaks five languages.

"Five languages!" exclaims the man. "Does it speak Yiddish?"

"Sure," says the salesman.

The customer buys the parrot for his mother who lives on her own in the Bronx. He'll send her the parrot, it'll keep her company.

The next day he calls her up—

"Mom, how did you like the parrot I bought you?"

"Mmm, delicious!" she says.

"What do you mean delicious?"

"I made soup out of it, came out great!"

"But mom, this was a special parrot – it spoke five languages!"

"So why didn't it say anything?"

***

Why were the Ten Commandments written on two separate tablets? God offered them first to the Germans.

"Impossible!" they cried. "What's all this about Thou Shalt not Kill. Killing is natural, we cannot accept!"

So God offered them to the French. "Unbelievable!" they said. "A law against adultery is against human nature." And they refused.

So God offered them to the Jews, who didn't read them but asked "How much do they cost?"

"They're free," came the reply.

"In that case we'll take two!"

***

Two Jewish businessmen went on safari together and while their wives were back at the lodge eating cakes and sipping tea, Joe and Alfie went for a walk in the bush. As they were going under a dense thicket of trees a large, hairy animal dropped from the branches and buried its teeth in Alfie's neck.

"Aaaarrrgh!" he screamed. "What is it?"

"How should I know?" said Joe. "You're the furrier!"

***

Two friends met in the street for the first time in many years.

"Morrie! How are you?"

"Fine, Bennie, terrific, and how's yourself and the family?"

"Wonderful! Listen, my Joe is getting married next week at the Walm Lane synagogue and I want you to come. Afterwards there's a reception at the Synagogue Hall, you know it? No? Well, you take the third on the left past the synagogue, second on the right past the laundry and number 32 is the Hall and you can ring the bell with your elbows!"

"Ring with my elbows?"

"Of course, you're coming with presents!"

***

***

Ginsberg returns home from a business trip to find out that his wife has been unfaithful to him. Very upset, he interrogates her.

"Was it that heap of dung, Goldberg?"

"No."

"Was it that pile of filth, Feigenbaum?"

"No."

"Was it that mountain of manure, Finklestein?"

"No."

"Was it that noxious bag of goat mess, Levy?"

"No!"

"What's the matter with my friends? Not good enough for you?"

***

A Jew was tottering drunkenly down the street when he bumped into a lamppost.

He swore at it: "Antisemite!"

***

Levy and Cohen were business competitors who also competed for luxuries and when car phones first came into fashion Levy got one immediately and phoned Cohen from his car to show off. Cohen worked like mad and saved every penny for a year, eventually getting a phone installed in his car. The first drive he made with it he rang Levy in his car to show off.

"Hi! Levy, how are you doing? I'm phoning from the car."

"Great, Cohen, but can I ring you back in a moment? I'm on the other line!"

***

Solly took his beautiful secretary out to dinner at a nice restaurant and took her back to her flat afterwards for coffee. Then he grew amorous and eventually managed to coax her to the bedroom. But once there no matter what he tried, he could not get an erection. Eventually, after acute embarrassment and profuse apologies, he went home.

There, sliding into bed next to his fat, snoring wife, her thigh touched his and he had an erection. Shaking his head in disgust, he got out of bed, looked at his erect organ and said, "Now I know why they call you a schmock!"

***

A rabbi and his friend the priest are locked in a fierce theological disagreement.

"Nonsense, Rabbi Bloom! Of course making love is work and not pleasure. It's God's work, in fulfilment of his Law."

"No, no," said the rabbi. "It's a pleasure, otherwise the human race would not have survived."

They agreed to consult their superiors and meet again in a month.

"Well, it's settled," said the priest. "I consulted the Bishop and he consulted the Archbishop and he consulted the Cardinal and we all agree – it's work!"

"Nonsense!" argued the rabbi. "The Chief Rabbi agreed with me: if it was work we'd make the maid do it."

***

Solly and Esther Ginsberg have been trying to become members of their local golf course for years, but without success and for obvious reasons. When her husband died and left her some money, Esther had a nose job, changed her name to Davina Lonsdale-Gordon and was eventually elected to membership.

For her first dinner at the club she wore a gorgeous new gown but as the waiter was serving her he poured some soup over her. Horrified, she stood up and yelled.

"Oy vey!" And hurriedly added, "Whatever that may mean."

***

***

There was a very long queue outside the Pearly Gates, everybody waiting their turn patiently. Then a grand looking man barged his way to the head of the queue and pushed his way through the gates.

There was much muttering of discontent.

"Who was that?" someone asked St Peter.

"Oh, that was God – he's fine most of the time but sometimes he thinks he's a doctor!"

***

Morrie and Beckie are in bed.

"Beckie," complains Morrie. "Shut the damned window! It's freezing outside!"

"And?" answered Beckie. "If I shut the window will it be warm outside?"

***

A Catholic priest, an Anglican parson and a rabbi were walking through the back streets of their town after an ecumenical meeting at a local hall. They were all horrified to see, through lit and un-curtained windows, a couple making love.

After a careful look the priest said there was no doubt about it but the offending couple were not of his flock.

"How do you know?" asked the other two.

"Simple – no crucifix on the wall."

The parson took a look and came to the same conclusion – they weren't of his flock either.

"How do you know?" asked the others.

"Easy – no bible on the shelves."

The rabbi had a look in and returned looking shamefaced.

"I'm afraid they are definitely from my congregation."

"How do you know?" asked the others.

"Fitted carpets."

★★★

It's the Day of Atonement, Yom Kippur, and on the bima, the central dais in the synagogue, the rabbi is beating his breast and wailing that he is truly insignificant in the eyes of the Lord. At his side the cantor is also beating his breast and uttering low moans as he bewails the fact that he is but a miserable speck on the face of God's creation. A little further away the shammus, or beadle, is tugging his beard and weeping very loudly that he is but a mote of insignificant dust in the Lord's universe.

The cantor turns to the rabbi and says: "Hmmm! Look at him, saying he's nothing!"

Two smart ladies meet in the street.

"Sylvie, you're looking wonderful! What have you been up to?"

"Guess what, Molly! I'm having an affair!"

"Fantastic! Who's doing the catering?"

★★★

★★★

A marriage broker in a small Ukrainian village is trying to persuade the young man of the virtues of his intended and the wealth of her parents. But the boy is incredulous.

"Don't you think they might have borrowed all that silver, just to impress me?"

"No way! Who would lend silver to such thieves!"

★★★

A Jew returning to Russia tried to smuggle in two sacks of coffee (a highly taxed item in Russia) at Moscow airport. The customs officers immediately found it.

"It's bird food," he protested as he was dragged away.

"Bird food?" cried the officer in charge, "you're crazy. It's coffee and birds don't eat coffee!"

"Look," the man replied. "If they like it they'll eat it, if they don't they won't!"

***

During the Nazi period in Germany Moishe Cohen walks into a Munich police station carrying a newspaper with an ad for a job with the police.

"What?" cried the officer in charge. "You a Jew, applying for a job with the Bavarian police, the vanguard of the Aryan nation? Out of here, Semitic scum! Are you crazy?"

"No, no," explained Moishe, "I just wanted to come in and reassure you that on me you shouldn't count!"

***

***

What a disaster! Morrie Goldberg spent the whole of Yom Kippur with a magnificent whore. He had met the voluptuous brunette at a trade reception and spent three days at a hotel with her. In the evening of the third day, Yom Kippur itself, Morrie, all bleary-eyed in bed, sat up suddenly and shouted "Mine God! What have I done? It's Yom Kippur!"

He got dressed in a trice, peeled off a wad of banknotes for the girl, kissed her goodbye and fled.

On his way home he passed a United Synagogue (strictly orthodox). He burst in and cornered the rabbi and burst out:

"Rabbi! Rabbi! I missed Yom Kippur! It's terrible! I completely forgot!"

"You forgot Yom Kippur! Oy veh! How?"

"I-I-oh God! I was with a woman."

"A woman? You mean your mother? Your wife?"

"No, no, a professional, a tart, a whore!"

"What? You abandoned God and repentance for a prostitute on Yom Kippur?"

"Yes, rabbi, and I'll do anything to repent!"

"My God! I must think about this and consult the Rabbinical Court. In the meantime you must go home and prostrate yourself for a week, eat nothing but dried bread once a day and water and pray for forgiveness all day and learn 80 psalms by heart. Return here in a week and I will have your punishment worked out."

Morrie crept out of the synagogue utterly crestfallen. What shame and humiliation – and a week without food and drink! On the way home he passed a Liberal synagogue and, on an impulse, went inside and found the rabbi.

"Rabbi!" he blurted out. "I must tell you, I missed Yom Kippur!"

"Missed Yom Kippur? That's serious. How did you do it?"

"I was with a woman," moaned Morrie.

"Really? Tell me about her."

"She wasn't my wife, or my mother, or my sister – she was a tall voluptuous whore! What can I do to repent?"

"Well, I'd better consult my colleagues, but for a start you'd better skip lunch…"

"Skip lunch? The rabbi at the United Synagogue told me to fast for a week – and that was to be just the beginning!"

"United synagogue? United Synagogue! What do they know about sex?"

***

In the old, now vanished Jewish communities of Central and East Europe, the Jews of Chelm were considered very stupid and served as the butt of "stupid" jokes for other Jews – just as the Americans joke about Poles, the French about Belgians, the British about the Irish and the Irish about the people from Kerry.

***

Shmuel goes to the post office with a parcel to send to his mother in Chelm.

"The parcel's too heavy," the post clerk told him. "You must put on more stamps."

"Gosh!" replied Shmuel in wonder. "Will that make the parcel lighter?"

***

Abie the butcher is walking down Chelm's main street when a man suddenly leaps out at him and wallops him. "There!" he shouts at Abie. "Take that, Moishe, and that! And that!" And wallops him again.

Abie eventually breaks free and laughs at the man who had been hitting him.

"Ha! Ha! The joke's on you! Ha! Ha! I'm not called Moishe, I'm Abie!"

***

***

Yossel sat next to Shmuel at the back of the Chelm synagogue. Every few minutes Shmuel shuffled his feet and winced in pain.

"What's the matter Shmuel?" asked Yossel.

"It's my feet, they're killing me. My shoes are too small."

"Then why not get a pair the right size and spare the rest of us your moans and groans?"

"I'll tell you why. My wife, Sadie, complains of rheumatism all night and won't let me get near her. Two weeks ago I lost my job and I can't pay the bills and my son has abandoned his studies though it cost me my life's savings to put him into university. But when I take my shoes off life seems wonderful!"

***

Two men from Chelm were going to see the rabbi when it started raining.

"Shmulik, put up your umbrella, it's raining."

"No point, Mendele, it's got holes in it."

"Then why did you bring it?"

"I didn't think it would rain!"

Dorothy Parker

Katherine Hepburn ran the whole gamut of emotions from A to B.

I'm the toast of two continents – Greenland and Australia

You can lead a horticulture but you can't make her think.

The only ism Hollywood believes in is plagiarism.

***

"I'm afraid you're going to need a lot of treatment and the fee will be $2000." Said Dr Carruthers to the unfortunate Goldberg.

"Doctor, I'm not a wealthy man and business is terrible!"

"OK, I'll reduce it, in view of your circumstances to $1700."

"Doctor! Give me a break, I've got three children to support."

"OK! OK!" sighed the doctor, "I'll make it $1500!"

"Doctor, couldn't you make it a little less – my mother's been ill too and I had to help her out!"

"OK! Make it $1400 but why on earth did you contact me? I'm one of the most expensive specialists in New York!"

"Listen," said Goldberg. "When it comes to my health money's no object!"

***

Joe meets Louis in the street.

"I've got a bargain for you," says Joe, "I can get you an elephant for only £50!"

"And what do I want from an elephant?" asks Louis. "I live on the third floor of a rickety old house and six of us share two rooms!"

"OK! You win," sighs Joe, "you can have two for £70!"

"Right! It's a deal!"

***

A famous art critic calls on Ivor Dalrymple (formerly Izzy Feigenbaum) who had amassed a famous collection of pictures including three fine Raphaels. But the critic was astonished when he examined the Raphaels closely – the standard signature of Rafaello in the bottom right hand corner had vanished and instead they were signed Rebecca.

"Why on earth are your Raphaels signed Rebecca?" he asked Dalrymple.

"Ah! That's the taxman's fault – I had to put them in my wife's name!"

***

★★★

Ginsberg's life went so catastrophically wrong that he had a mental breakdown and was admitted to an asylum for the insane. He insisted on kosher food. They offered him a meals-on-wheels service but he insisted on eating in the canteen with the other patients. After much hassle and expense the hospital gave in to his unreasonable demands and served kosher food in the canteen just for Ginsberg, their only Jewish patient.

After a few weeks the chief psychiatrist was walking through the restaurant and he saw Ginsberg tucking into a large plate of bacon and eggs.

The doctor was outraged. "But Ginsberg! I thought you only ate kosher food!"

"Ha! Doctor! You've forgotten! I'm meshuggah (mad)!"

★★★

Levy comes home unexpectedly during the day and finds his wife in bed with Goldberg. "What on earth are you doing?" he yells at them both. "See!" says Levy's wife to Goldberg, "I told you he was stupid!"

★★★

An old Jew asks his grandson to explain Einstein's theory of relativity to him.

"Well, it's like this, grandpa. He reckoned that an hour at the dentist seems longer than an hour in a good restaurant."

"Hmmm, and from this he makes a living?"

★★★

A notice in a synagogue read: Come early if you want to get a seat at the back.

***

Sam was driving along when his car was stopped by a policeman. "Are you aware that a woman, presumably your wife, fell out of your car five miles back?"

Sam replies, "Thank God for that, I thought I'd gone deaf!"

***

How do we know Jesus was a Jew? Simple. He lived at home till he was thirty, he went into his father's business, his mother thought he was God and he thought she was a virgin.

***

Overheard in the urinal of a well-known London synagogue:

"Ah! I see you were circumcised by blind old Rabbi Feigenbaum."

"How do you know?"

"You're peeing on my right foot!"

***

***

Beckie said to Benny:

"Benny, the bank manager's on the phone."

"Yes, Mr Carruthers, what can I do for you?"

"You're £700 overdrawn, Mr Cohen."

"And what was the position last month?"

"Last month? Why, you were £250 in credit."

"So! And did I ring you?"

***

A man started to tell a joke at a party: "Two old Jews were on their way…"

Suddenly, he was interrupted by a sensitive guest. "Tell me, why do so many jokes begin with Jews?"

"OK, I'm sorry," apologised the story teller. "I'll start again. Two old Chinese men were on their way to see the Rabbi at the synagogue…"

When Sir Moses Montefiore was told by another guest at a London dinner party that Japan was a happy country because it contained neither pigs nor Jews, he said: "In that case you and I should both go as Japan would then have one of each."

★★★

Ginsberg says to Goldberg, who is also a small businessman: "Tell me, why do you keep knocking down old Cohen's prices? You know you're not going to pay him anyway."

"He's a nice man, that Cohen," Goldberg replies. "I'm trying to keep down his losses!"

★★★

***

Goldberg meets Ginsberg on the way into the synagogue for Sabbath prayers

"Funny," says Goldberg, "you always ask me how my family is but never how my business is doing."

"So how's business?"

"Don't ask!"

***

Morrie was on his death bed.

"Sarah," he croaked. "Are you there?"

"I'm here Morrie, I'm here."

"Wilbur, you there?"

"I'm, here, Poppa, I'm right here."

Silence.

"Milton, you here too?"

"Yes, Dad, I'm here, of course."

Morrie jerked himself up on his elbow and yelled:

"So who's minding the shop?"

***

***

Three men are struggling through the desert on foot.

The first, a Frenchman, cries, "I'm so thirsty, I must have a cold glass of Chablis!"

The second, an Englishman, says, "I'm so thirsty I must have a glass of scotch and soda on ice!"

The third, a Jew, says, "I'm so thirsty, I must have diabetes!"

***

An aspiring young Jewish actor, straight out of drama school, goes for his first audition, at the BBC in London. He gets the part and, overjoyed, he dashes home to tell his mother the great news.

"Guess what, Mummy! I got the part!"

"Which part?" she asks.

"You know, Mum! The part I was after. The husband."

"The husband? What? You couldn't get a talking part?"

***

What does a Frenchwoman say when she's making love?

"Ah! C'est merveilleux!"

What does an Italian woman say?

"Ah! Che maravigliosa!"

What does a Jewish woman say?

"Sam! The ceiling needs painting!"

Maureen Lipman

A Jewish Nymphomaniac is a woman who will sleep with a man on the same day as she has her hair done.

***

A poor Jew is walking down the street when he
sees a funeral of a rich man – a black Rolls
Royce, lots of well-dressed guests, tons of
flowers. He shakes his head:

"Now that's what I call living."

***

Fifteen minutes after the *Titanic* sank Morrie
and Louie find themselves hanging on to the
same piece of wood. "Well," said Louie, "it could
have been worse."

"Oh, how?" asked Morrie.

"We could have bought return tickets!"

***

A man calls out to the waiter in a Jewish
restaurant: "Excuse me, do you have matzoh
balls?"

"No, I always walk like this."

***

A Jew asks an orthodox rabbi to say a brocha (a blessing) over his new Ferrari.

"What's a Ferrari?" asks the rabbi and refuses.

So he approaches a Reform rabbi, who asks: "What's a brocha?"

***

Did you hear the Jewish kamakaze pilot?
He crashed his plane into his father's scrap metal yard.

***

Two men are sharing a train compartment, one Jewish, one not. Every few minutes the Jew rocks to and fro and beats his breast and mutters, "oy, oy, oy."

Eventually, exasperated, the Gentile asks him what on earth is the matter.

"Oy, oy, oy – am I on the wrong train!"

***

A Jewish doctor gave his patient six months to live and sent his bill. When the man didn't pay he gave him another six months.

***